Cover design by Justin Watkinson

ISBN: 978-0-7643-6477-8
Printed in China

Published by Schiffer Publishing, Ltd.
4880 Lower Valley Road
Atglen, PA 19310
Phone: (610) 593-1777; Fax: (610) 593-2002
Email: Info@schifferbooks.com
Web: www.schifferbooks.com

For our complete selection of fine books on this and related subjects, please visit our website at www.schifferbooks.com. You may also write for a free catalog.

Schiffer Publishing's titles are available at special discounts for bulk purchases for sales promotions or premiums. Special editions, including personalized covers, corporate imprints, and excerpts, can be created in large quantities for special needs. For more information, contact the publisher.

We are always looking for people to write books on new and related subjects. If you have an idea for a book, please contact us at proposals@schifferbooks.com.

Acknowledgments

Beyond the invaluable help provided by the staffs of the National Archives, the Bundesarchiv, and the Patton Museum, I am indebted to Tom Kailbourn, the late Walter Spielberger, Thomas Anderson, Dana Bell, Chris Hughes, Scott Taylor, Hans-Heiri Stapfer, Tom Laemlein, and the late Massimo Foti. Their generous and skillful assistance adds immensely to the quality of this volume. On this project and in all aspects of my life, I am especially blessed to have the faithful and tireless help of my wonderful wife, Denise, who has scanned countless photos and documents for this and numerous other books.

Contents

INTRODUCTION:
A Less Celebrated Cat

The Soviet T-34 was directly responsible for the creation of the Panther. This then-new Soviet tank outclassed the German Panzer III and Panzer IV vehicles, which previously had the decided advantage on the battlefield. The T-34 had better firepower, protection, and mobility, and the German forces demanded a tank that not only equaled the T-34, but bettered it. *Bundesarchiv*

Even though the Panzerkampfwagen V has never received the attention or respect lavished on the much-feared Tiger tank, the "Panther" was arguably the more effective of Germany's World War II–era armored cats.

The Panther was introduced in 1943 as Germany's new medium tank, intended to replace both the Panzer III and Panzer IV—both of which had been outclassed by the Soviet T-34 (medium) and KV-I (heavy) tanks.

The Panther offered an outstanding combination of firepower, armored protection, and mobility for the era. Even so, the early Panzer Vs were plagued with mechanical issues, many of which were the result of the vehicles being rushed into production and then into service for the Kursk offensive during the summer of 1943.

Some issues, such as crew training, were improved within a few months. Panther tank operational rates climbed from just 16 percent in July 1943 to nearly 40 percent by December. Unfortunately, certain mechanical issues, most notably problems with the transmission, continued to plague the Panther to the end of the war. These issues were compounded by the Allied bombing that impacted tank assembly plants, as well as the factories that produced key parts and subassemblies.

Other problems for the Panther arose from the use of slave labor to manufacture vehicles and their components. To help reduce the 117,100-Reichsmark cost per tank, Germany impressed prisoners of war as industrial workers. A 1947 study showed that these POWs frequently and effectively sabotaged the weapons systems they worked on, resulting in frequent breakdowns and a shortened service life.

Nearly eighty years past its introduction, the Panther still has a modern appearance. The sloping glacis plate, designed to deflect armor-piercing shot and increase the overall effectiveness of the frontal armor, creates one of the most distinctive profiles among World War II AFVs.

The Panther was originally designed as a 30-ton vehicle, with its engine and transmission sized accordingly, but the Panther's weight quickly began to climb, ultimately growing to nearly 45 tons and overloading the chassis and power train.

MAN and Daimler-Benz submitted proposals for a new tank based on lessons learned with the Soviet T-34. The Daimler-Benz VK 3002 proposal, a model of which is shown here, obviously owed more to the T-34's design than MAN's winning proposal.

This is the second of two Panther prototypes produced by MAN in the fall of 1942. The first prototype was an automotive test vehicle and lacked a turret. Known as Versuchs-Panthers, the drive sprocket of the prototypes differed considerably from those used on production vehicles. *Thomas Anderson collection*

Specifications			
	Ausf. D	**Ausf.**	**A Ausf. G**
Length	8.86 meters	8.86 meters	8.86 meters
Width	3.27 meters	3.42 meters	3.42 meters
Height	2.99 meters	3.10 meters	3.10 meters
Weight	44.8 metric tons	45.5 metric tons	45.5 metric tons
Fuel Capacity	730 liters	730 liters	700 liters
Maximum Speed	55 km/hr	55 km/hr	46 km/hr
Range, On Road	200 km	200 km	200 km
Range, Cross Country	100 km	100 km	100 km
Crew	5	5	5
Communications	Fu 5 and Fu 2, Intercom	Fu 5 and Fu 2, Intercom	Fu 5 and Fu 2, Intercom
Chassis Numbers			
M.A.N.	210001–210254	210255–210899	120301–121443(apx.)
Daimler-Benz	211001–211250	151901–152575	124301–125304(apx.)
Henschel	212001–212130	---	---
M.N.H.	213001–213220	154801–155630	128301–129114
Demag	---	158101–158150	---
Weapon, Main	7.5 cm KwK 42 L/70	7.5 cm KwK 42 L/70	7.5 cm KwK 42 L/70
Elevation	−8° to +18°	−8° to +18°	−8° to +18°
Weapon, Secondary	7.92 mm MG 34	7.92 mm MG 34	7.92 mm MG 34
In Hull	7.92 mm MG 34	7.92 mm MG 34	7.92 mm MG 34
Ammo Stowage, Main	79 rounds	79 rounds	82 rounds
Ammo Stowage, Secondary	5,100 rounds	5,100 rounds	4,800 rounds
Armor, Glacis	80 mm / 55°	80 mm / 55°	80 mm / 55°
Armor, Hull Side	40 mm / 0°	40 mm / 0°	40 mm / 0°
Gun Mantlet	100 mm	100 mm	100–110 mm
Turret Front	100 mm / 12°	100 mm / 12°	100 mm / 12°
Turret Side/Rear	45 mm / 25°	45 mm / 25°	45 mm / 25°
Engine Make, Config.	Maybach V-12	Maybach V-12	Maybach V-12
Engine Model	HL230 TRM P30	HL230 TRM P30	HL230 TRM P30
Engine Displacement	23 liters	23 liters	23 liters
Engine Horsepower	650 @ 3,000 rpm	700 @ 3,000 rpm	600 @ 2,500 rpm

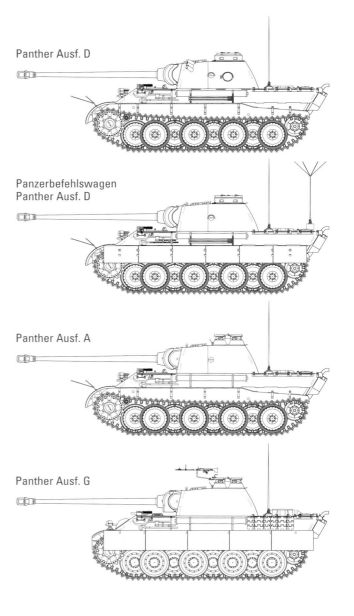

Panther Ausf. D

Panzerbefehlswagen Panther Ausf. D

Panther Ausf. A

Panther Ausf. G

CHAPTER 1
Panther D: First of the Breed

The first model of the Panther to come off the assembly line was the Ausführung, or model, D. One thousand of the new tanks had been ordered from Maschinenfabrik Augsburg-Nürnberg (MAN), Daimler-Benz, Maschinenfabrik Niedersachsen-Hannover (MNH), and Henschel und Sohn in Kassel. Interestingly, Henschel would build only chassis, using turrets produced by Wegman, also in Kassel. The other firms would produce both chassis and turrets.

Before the first tank of the initial one-thousand-unit order was completed, the production number had been reduced to 850 units. This was in part due to the diversion of some chassis for Bergepanther recovery vehicle production, but ultimately only 842 Panther Ausf. Ds were completed as combat tanks.

Despite Adolf Hitler's insistence on quick production, the first Panthers were not completed until January 1943, when the four firms involved finished twenty-six vehicles. The Panther's combat debut was further delayed by the discovery of various problems with the new design, most notably with the engines.

There were ninety-six of the new tanks issued to Panzer-Abteilung 51, operating on the Eastern Front on June 24, 1943. A few days later, a further ninety-six Panthers (plus two Bergepanthers) were issued to the nearby Panzer-Abteilung 52. By July 5, the Panthers were in action during the Battle of Kursk. As revealed in a report by Generaloberst Heinz Guderian, then "Inspekteur der Panzertruppen," submitted to the chief of staff, after just two days in action, only forty Panthers remained operational. After five days this figure had dropped to a mere ten vehicles. Twenty-five were total losses, while fifty-six had been damaged in combat, and forty-four had broken down. The remainder littered the battlefield, their condition unknown.

An early Panther Ausf. D from the 4th Platoon, 4th Company, Panzer-Regiment Großdeutschland, bears colors and markings used during fighting near Karachev, Russia, in 1943.

The first production model of the Panther tank was the Ausführung D (Ausf. D) ("model D"), the first of which were completed in January 1943 following a brief, nine-month development and initial production period. The Panther Ausf. D made use of an existing but modified Rheinmetall turret, mounting a powerful 7.5 cm Kampfwagenkanone KwK 42 L/70 gun. The hull incorporated sloped armor to increase the protective properties of the plate. The driver had a vision port with a hinged cover: a feature that carried over to the next production model, the Ausf. A. Seen here are Panther Ausf. Ds in overall Dunkelgelb (dark yellow) camouflage paint, being prepared for shipment by railroad flatcars in 1943. *Bundesarchiv*

Workers on the Henschel & Sohn assembly line in Kassel appear oblivious to the several tons of Panther Ausf. D hull passing over their heads in June 1943. Once welded together, the hull was machined for installation of the various components prior to beginning its trip down the final assembly line. *Bundesarchiv*

A Panther Ausf. D undergoes analysis at a proving ground. The light-colored rectangle on the upper right corner of the glacis contains the number 1A-0805. This vehicle was completed after June 1943, as indicated by the presence of only one headlight. *Patton Museum*

Crews load Panther Ausf. Ds onto flatcars for shipment to the front. Protective bundles of sticks have been wrapped around the 7.5 cm gun barrels on the first two tanks. *NARA*

Factory and military representatives pose next to Panther Ausf. D chassis number 210111 at the Maschinenfabrik Augsburg-Nürnberg (MAN) factory after it was remanufactured with the latest improvements in June 1943. "KV" stood for combat ready (*Kriegsverwendungsfähig*), and this tank was the first tank to come out of the program. *Hans-Heiri Stapfer collection*

The crew of a Panther Ausf. D pauses on an Eastern Front road march in June or July 1943. Between the two storage boxes on the engine deck is an armored hood that covers the opening for a telescoping snorkel for deepwater fording. *Bundesarchiv*

In a view from about the same time and place as the preceding image, the commander of a Panther Ausf. D scans the sky with his binoculars in search of Soviet aircraft. The cylinder on the sponson contains a bore-cleaning brush and staff. *Bundesarchiv*

In August or September 1943, the crew of a Panther Ausf. D makes repairs to the final drive and the left track of their vehicle at a site near the Mius River in the Donets Basin in the southern USSR. Track repairs and changes typically were very arduous tasks. *Bundesarchiv*

A member of the crew of a Panther Ausf. D poses in the rear hatch of the turret, somewhere in northern France in the fall of 1943. This photo provides a rare, close-up study of Zimmerit as applied to a Panther Ausf. D. Tactical number "425" is painted on the cupola. *Bundesarchiv*

The drum-shaped early-style cupola on the turret marks this Panther as an Ausf. D. Further proof of the model of Panther is the chassis number, 212080, painted on the front of the headlight cover. This was one of the 130 Panther Ausf. Ds produced by Henchel, all of which were completed in 1943. Details of the Zimmerit application are apparent. *Patton Museum*

This is the same Panther Ausf. D seen in the preceding photograph, as viewed from the rear. On the jack is painted in white the number "80," which may represent the last two digits of chassis number 212080. A lateral bracket supported the two exhaust pipes above the mufflers. The cupola is fitted with a ring mount for a machine gun. *Patton Museum*

As seen in a third and final photo of the same Panther Ausf. D, additional sections of spare track have been attached to the sponson and turret. Zimmerit is present on the armored skirts, and a metal ladder is attached to the skirt to the far right. *Patton Museum*

A Panther advances along a dusty road in the Soviet Union during the warm months of 1943. The drum-type commander's cupola identifies this as an Ausf. D tank. The dark, oblong feature on the right rear of the turret is the interlock with the rear plate of the turret. *Bundesarchiv*

A Panther Ausf. D accompanies motorized troops through a village. It is equipped with armor skirts, for extra protection for the 40 mm side armor of the hull. The pistol-port plug on the side of the turret has been detached and is hanging from a retainer chain. *Patton Museum*

The crews of two Panther Ausf. Ds take a break on a road march. The turret of the rear tank is traversed to the rear. On the right front corner of the turret roof of the closer Panther are spare track links, atop which sits a storage box with its lid ajar. *Bundesarchiv*

A Panther Ausf. D emerges from a forest while negotiating a muddy trail in the USSR during December 1943. The site was outside Kirovograd (now Kropyvnytskyi), in central Ukraine. The letterbox cover for the bow machine gun shows as an area that is relatively smoother than the mud-spattered glacis surrounding it. Faintly visible above the dual sight apertures on the left side of the turret is a curved rain gutter, introduced to Ausf. D production in June 1943. *Bundesarchiv*

An early-production Panther Ausf. D with smoke-grenade dischargers on the turret rests along the side of a road in the southern part of the Eastern Front in September 1943. A dark camouflage scheme has been applied at various places over the Dunkelgelb base color. A heat shield is visible on the inboard side of the left stowage bin on the rear of the hull. What appears to be a ladder is stored on the right side of the vehicle, and an improvised step made of a bent steel rod is attached to the next-to-rear skirt panel. *Bundesarchiv*

A Panther Ausf. D of Panzergrenadier Division "Großdeutschland" provides fire support on the Russian southern front in 1944. An armored hood for the telescoping snorkel, an Ausf. D feature, is on the engine deck to the front of the right exhaust pipe. *Bundesarchiv*

Two crewmen change a wheel on the left side of a Panther Ausf. D. On the bottom of the sponson are hangers for the armored skirts, which feature upturned tabs on the ends that were fastened through openings in the skirt panels. *Bundesarchiv*

A pair of Panthers Ausf. Ds are parked along a road in a forest in the northwestern Soviet Union in the winter of 1943–44, fir branches providing camouflage. The tank on the left, marked number "438" on the turret, may be identified as an Ausf. D instead of an A by the shape of the semicircular extension of the turret front behind the mantlet. *Bundesarchiv*

Panther Ausf. D

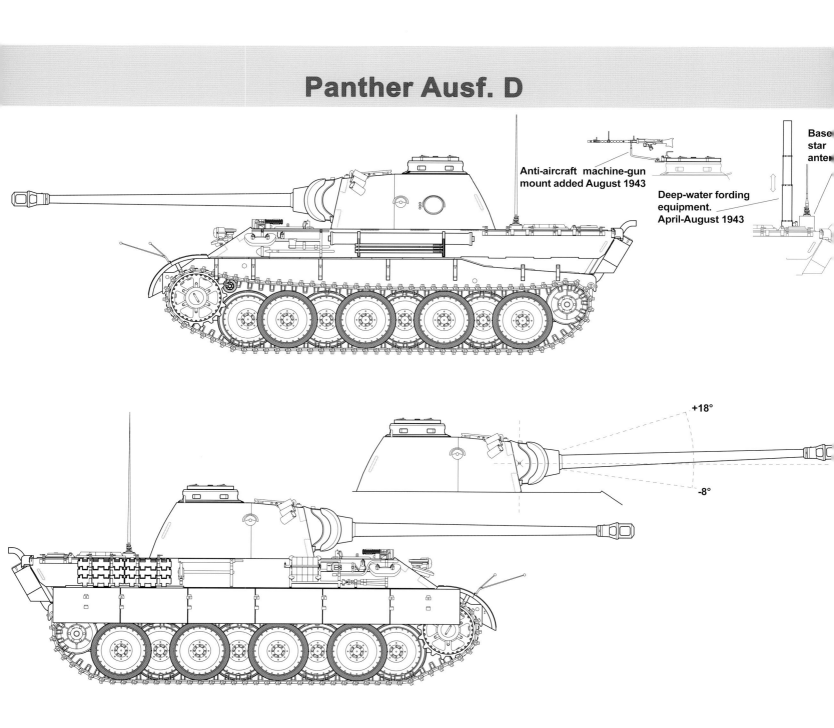

Anti-aircraft machine-gun mount added August 1943

Deep-water fording equipment. April-August 1943

Base star anten

+18°

-8°

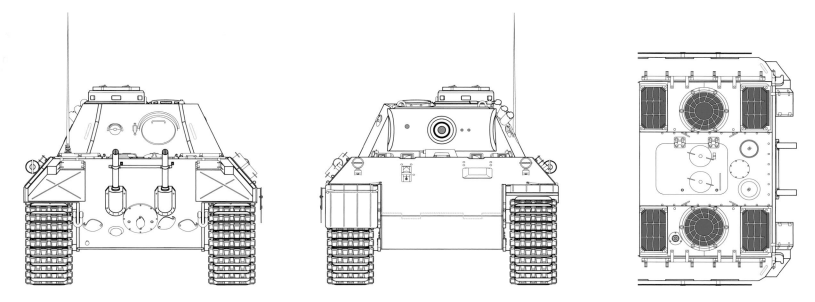

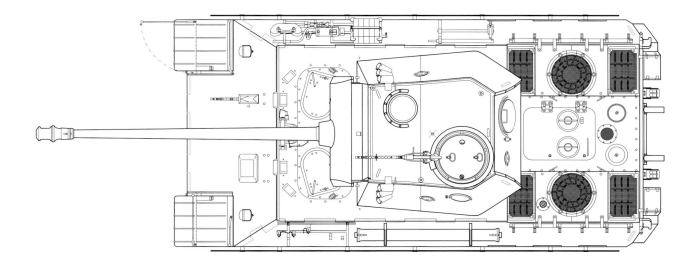

CHAPTER 2

Panther A:
The Midproduction Panther

The second model of the Panther to enter production was the Panther Ausf. A, which began to roll off the assembly lines in August 1943. While many of the original Panthers had been damaged or lost during the fighting at the Kursk salient, much of the fault had been placed on inadequate training and a lack of proper field trials as opposed to tank design.

While the Panther units had suffered considerably at Kursk, it should be noted that the Germans also claimed almost 300 Soviet tanks destroyed in return—including a T-34 knocked out at an amazing 3,000 meters.

The Panther A differed little, particularly in its external appearance, from the Panther Ausf. D. Internally, the initial hulls were identical in the Ausf. A and Ausf. D. The HL230TRM V-12 engine, which had replaced the HL210 after the first 250 Panther Ausf. Ds were

produced, continued to be used on the Ausf. A. Indeed, the HL230 would continue as the engine for all subsequent Panthers, although plans did call for the introduction of the fuel-injected HL234. The war ended before that engine entered production.

The Panther turret was extensively redesigned for the Ausf. A. Though the shape of the turret was little changed, most of the mechanics were revised. Initially, the turret retained the same type of drum cupola found on the Ausf. D, but a cast commander's cupola featuring seven periscopes quickly replaced the older drum style. In late 1943, the hull was changed, and the familiar Panther ball-mounted MG 34 machine gun replaced the initial "letterbox"-style firing port on the glacis plate. Ultimately, 2,200 of the Ausf. A tanks were produced from August 1943 through August 1944.

A particular feature that differentiated the Panther Ausf. A from the Ausf. D was the shape of the D-shaped armor extensions on the front of the turret, which snugly fit to the rear of the mantlet. *Walter Spielberger*

232981

With production spanning from August 1943 to July 1944, the Panther Ausf. A essentially consisted of the Panther Ausf. D chassis coupled with an improved turret. This example built by Maschinenfabrik Augsburg-Nürnberg (MAN), on whose factory grounds it was photographed, has the cast cupola and Zimmerit, the latter being applied to the Ausf. A in late August or early September 1943. Although the drum-shaped cupola of the Ausf. D seems to have been installed on the first few Ausf. A tanks, by September 1943 it had been replaced by a new, cast cupola with seven periscopes: the cupola with which this tank is equipped. For the first few months of production by MAN, the Ausf. A shared the Ausf. D's "letterbox" cover for the bow MG 34 machine gun aperture and binocular gunsight apertures in the mantlet. The mantlet, however, was now noticeably wider. Three pistol ports initially were fitted on the turret, but these were omitted beginning in December 1943, in favor of the roof-mounted Nahverteidigungswaffe or "close-defense weapon." The Nahverteidigungswaffe was originally developed as a smoke grenade launcher, but a time-delay explosive round was developed for it, allowing it to defend an area of 20–30 feet around the tank. *Walter Spielberger*

As seen on the same Panther Ausf. A in the photo on page 17, the monocular gunsight aperture on the mantlet to the left side of the 7.5 cm gun and the ball-type bow-machine-gun mount, modifications dating to November 1943, were visible departures from the Ausf. D. *Walter Spielberger*

Except for the use of a cast cupola instead of a drum-shaped cupola, the MAN Panther Ausf. A featured here and in the two photos above appears from the rear virtually identical to a late-production Ausf. D. The jack is stored below the exhausts. *Walter Spielberger*

At the front of the side of the hull of this Ausf. A chassis under construction at the MAN factory is the mounting for the left final-drive assembly. On the side armor above the mounting is the elongated tab where it interlocks with the glacis. Just below the mounting and at intervals on the lower part of the side are access plates for the torsion bar mountings. Above the second access plate are five threaded studs for holding a bump stop. The first, second, and seventh road-wheel arms are reinforced. *Patton Museum*

On another Panther Ausf. A chassis on the MAN assembly line, the left final-drive assembly and most of the road wheels have been installed. The small roller with the black rubber tire attached to the final drive was intended to prevent the track from bunching up on the sprocket when the vehicle was being driven in reverse. On the side of the lower hull, Zimmerit with a vertically ridged texture has been applied over the light-colored material seen in the preceding photograph, that material apparently being an initial, fairly smooth coat of Zimmerit to give the final coat some tooth to adhere to. The textured Zimmerit was kept away from the suspension and final drive. *Patton Museum*

The sprocket, idler, and all of the road wheels are installed on this Panther Ausf. A chassis at the MAN factory. Also present are the tool rack toward the front of the sponson and the tubular container for the bore-cleaning brush and staff on the center of the sponson. Vertically ribbed Zimmerit is on the sides of the lower hull and sponson. *Patton Museum*

In the front interior of a Panther Ausf. A chassis under construction, the opening for the driver's visor and the ball mount are toward the top, steering brakes and the right front shock absorber are to the sides, and torsion bars are at the bottom. *Patton Museum*

Zimmerit has been applied to the glacis of this Panther Ausf. A at the MAN factory. The pattern of the Zimmerit features grids several inches square, within which are vertical ridges. Zimmerit is absent in the ball mount and driver's visor. *Patton Museum*

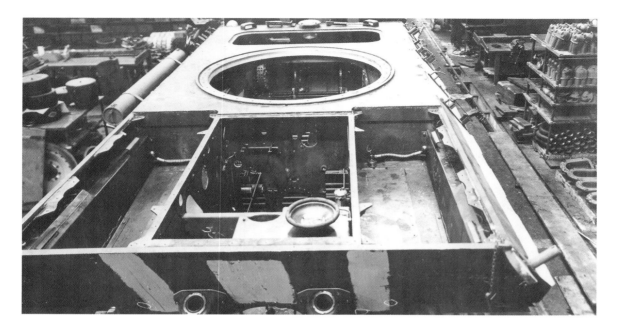

The five fuel tanks are in place on this Panther Ausf. A. Each sponson holds a tank whose outboard side is angled to match the armor's slope, with another tank below it. In the rear of the center bay is a tank with a bowl-shaped fuel filler atop it. *Patton Museum*

Viewed from above the turret opening, the Maybach HL230 P30 V-12 gasoline engine has been installed in the center compartment of a Panther Ausf. A, and the water coolers and fans have been emplaced in the upper parts of the side bays. *Patton Museum*

The fan and water-cooler grilles on the engine deck of Panzerbefehlswagen Panther Ausf. A, chassis number 210651, have screens to repel hand grenades and keep foreign objects from entering the engine compartment. The cylinder at the deck's rear is the guard for the star-antenna base. *Patton Museum*

Fliegerbeschußgerät

A Panzerbefehlswagen Panther Ausf. A turret before installation shows the turret floor, supports, and other structures. Zimmerit is on the mantlet and turret sides and front. The ring mount for a machine gun on the cupola was instituted on August 1, 1943. *Patton Museum*

A Panther Ausf. A from an unidentified unit negotiates a very rough piece of terrain in a clearing in Italy in 1944. The tube on the sponson for storing the bore-cleaning staff for the main gun is well battered, being made of relatively thin sheet metal. *Bundesarchiv*

This Panther A, tactical number "324," is evidently the same one in the preceding photo and is seen as it maneuvers over difficult terrain. The vehicle has Zimmerit, and two storage boxes have been mounted on short legs on the rear of the engine deck. *Bundesarchiv*

The white-outlined "R02" on the armor skirt of this Panther Ausf. A was the tactical number for a regimental executive officer in the unit. This vehicle has long been believed to be that of Hauptsturmführer Hans Gruhle of Leibstandarte SS "Adolf Hitler"; however, more recent research has attributed this as being a vehicle of the 3rd Panzer Regiment attached to the 2nd Panzer Division in Normandy. The color chips to the side of the profile depict the three colors of the camouflage, top to bottom: Olivgrün (olive green: RAL 6003), Dunkelgelb (dark yellow: RAL 7028), and Rotbraun (red brown: RAL 8017).

The Panther in the foreground is attempting to recover the bogged Panther in the background. The closer vehicle has MAN-type Zimmerit of vertical ridges in grids. Strapped above the sponson is a section of log, probably for unditching. *NARA*

The tactical number 613 is on the turret of this mud-spattered early Panther Ausf. A with MAN-type Zimmerit and a letterbox bow-machine-gun cover, the latter feature indicating the vehicle was completed before early December 1943. *NARA*

A Panther Ausf. A with the tactical number "221" on the turret maneuvers on a street in a village. The tank has the rough-textured Zimmerit associated with Daimler-Benz production and exhibits features appropriate to an Ausf. A completed up to November 1943, including the loader's periscope shield to the right of the cupola on the turret roof. The skirt panels have varying camouflage patterns and paint shades on them: a likely indication that they were scavenged from other vehicles.

Panther "221" from I./Panzer-Regiment 4 is shown in Liri Valley, Italy, 1944. This was an independent unit attached to the 26th Panzer Division, which was engaged in a futile effort to hold the so-called "Hitler Line" between Fondi and Terracina.

The commander of a MAN-produced Panzerbefehlswagen Panther Ausf. A looks warily to the rear as his tank advances. On the center rear of the engine deck are the star antenna and its armored base, features associated with this vehicle. *Patton Museum*

Panthers maintain a healthy space between them as they advance across a field. The nearest tank, an Ausf. A, features Zimmerit on the skirts as well as on the chassis and turret.

A column of Panther tanks proceeds along a deeply rutted, muddy road. The first two vehicles appear to be Panther Ausf. A tanks with ball-mount bow machine guns. Several of the skirt panels are missing from the lead tank, revealing the triangular piece of armor at the bottom of the sponson. The third Panther in the column has a letterbox-type cover for the bow machine gun, and the cupola is not clearly visible, so this could be a very late Ausf. D or an Ausf. A produced up to November 1943.

A Panther Ausf. A built by Daimler-Benz between December 1943 and May 1944 advances across a plain. The rough style of Daimler-Benz Zimmerit has been applied to the vehicle. There are no pistol ports in the turret; these were deleted in December 1943.

Whitewash has been applied overall to a late-production Panther Ausf. A serving with the 3rd Platoon, 8th Company, of a regiment in the 5th SS Panzer Division "Wiking" in Poland in 1944. The whitewash is relatively fresh, since the water-soluble finish tended to deteriorate when subjected to the elements.

A 1st SS Panzer Division Panther Ausf. A with Daimler-Benz-pattern Zimmerit veers around the Arc de Triomphe in Paris in the summer of 1944. This vehicle, produced between April and June 1944, has the two cooling pipes next to the left exhaust and a jack stored between the exhausts.

Two Panther Ausf. A tanks with Daimler-Benz Zimmerit are on adjacent flatcars at a rural railroad yard. Clear details are available of the muzzle cover issued with these tanks. The tank on the left has the monocular gunsight aperture in the mantlet.

Oberst (colonel) Willy Langkeit, second from left, Panzer Regiment "Großdeutschland" commander, rests with his crew by their Panther Ausf. A, tactical number "01," in Moldavia on May 17, 1944. The tank has the ball-type bow-machine-gun mount. *Patton Museum*

Crewmen refuel a Panther Ausf. A, well camouflaged by pine branches in a forest. Although difficult to discern, Zimmerit in the style applied by the MAN factory is present. This tank was produced between April and July 1944. *NARA*

A tow cable is attached to the rear of a Panther Ausf. A produced by MAN between December 1943 and March 1944. It features MAN-type Zimmerit and a jack between the exhausts and lacks pistol ports and cooling pipes next to the left exhaust. *NARA*

A Panther loaded on a railroad flatcar has received thorough whitewash camouflage. Even the C-type tow hook and the jack block on the side of the sponson have been whitewashed. Tactical number "511" is painted in white on a dark-colored patch. *Patton Museum*

A soldier is giving hand directions to the driver of a Panther Ausf. A tactical number "511," the same vehicle shown in the preceding photo. The barrel of the 7.5 cm gun was painted in a dark color. Cross-hatched Zimmerit is visible on the lower plate of the bow.

General Karl Lorenz, commander of Panzergrenadier Division "Grossdeutschland," confers with officers next to a Panzerbefehlswagen Panther Ausf. A at a command center in Ukraine in January 1944. The antenna on the turret roof is for an FuG 5 radio set. *Patton Museum*

In another photo of the same Panzerbefehlswagen Panther Ausf. A in the preceding photo, Willy Langkeit, commander of Panzer Regiment "Großdeutschland," in the cupola of this Panzerbefehlswagen Panther Ausf. A, confers with Gen. Hasso von Manteuffel, standing in a Schwimmwagen. *Patton Museum*

A German machine gunner with an MG 34 mans a foxhole next to a Panther Ausf. A. In the distance is a Sturmgeschütz III (StuG III). The Panther has a faded coat of whitewash. A dust cover is fitted over the 7.5 cm gun muzzle. There is Zimmerit on the skirts.

Horses drawing a supply cart have paused alongside a snow-plastered Panther Ausf. A while personnel in the background scan the terrain ahead. This is an MNH Panther produced between September and November 1943.

During a pause in wintertime fighting, crewmen of a Panther Ausf. A take advantage of the elevation of its engine deck and the protection of the turret to make observations. This MNH Panther has pistol ports and the letterbox bow-machine-gun mount.

The same Panther Ausf. A shown in the preceding photograph is seen from the right front as panzer personnel confer. Another Panther is in the background. The men are wearing a variety of hats and caps as well as reversible parkas with the white sides turned out.

Infantrymen, including a sniper next to the turret with a rifle with a scope, ride a 5th SS Panzer Division Panther Ausf. A in a posed photo. A crisscross camouflage pattern has been painted over the base color of the tank, through which a tactical number, "625," is faintly visible. This image, and the sequence following through page 50, illustrate 5 SS Panzer Division operations near Kovel, Poland in April 1944.

On a Panther Ausf. A maneuvering on a railroad embankment, a ball machine-gun mount is present but the turret roof lacks boom sockets and a close-defense weapon, narrowing down the production time frame to November 1943 to February 1944. *NARA*

A Panther Ausf. A crosses a muddy patch in a marshy area. The tank has a ball-mount bow machine gun, tactical number "622," and a metal debris guard over the mantlet, a feature usually associated with the Ausf. G.

Infantry troops are crouching on the engine deck of a Panther Ausf. A during a firefight. The tactical number "622" is in white on the side of the turret, and the vehicle has a subtle camouflage pattern of wavy lines over the Dunkelgelb base color. *NARA*

In a photo apparently related to the preceding one, a MAN Panther Ausf. A slogs through muddy ground. The vehicle has a ball-mounted bow machine gun and a monocular gunsight aperture on the mantlet: these two factors establish the vehicle's earliest production date from November 1943 to March 1944. The tank is equipped with six-chevron tracks, which would have provided slightly more traction than the smooth tracks in a swampy area such as this. *NARA*

In a rear view of the same Panther Ausf. A, tactical number "622," it can be seen that this vehicle had a pipe to each side of the left exhaust. These additional pipes, for cooling the left exhaust manifold during cold weather, were initiated on the Ausf. A in January 1944. *NARA*

Although the armor skirts obscure features that differentiate between the two cast-cupola Panthers, the Ausf. A and Ausf. G, this vehicle has two certain indicators of an Ausf. A: the single headlight on the left side of the glacis, the cover for the driver's vision port in the glacis, and the smaller-sized jack block. *NARA*

An infantryman in the foreground crouches next to a Panther Ausf. A with its 7.5 cm gun slightly depressed, ready to engage a nearby target. The Zimmerit is in grids with an apparently overall rough surface, in the style applied at the factory by Daimler-Benz. *NARA*

A Panther Ausf. A is positioned alongside a shed while two tanks, evidently Panthers, cross the field in the distance. This Panther exhibits MAN-style Zimmerit, including a radiating, ridged pattern on the outer edge of the 7.5 cm gun mantlet. *NARA*

German soldiers are gathered around a towed antitank gun that appears to be a captured Soviet 7.62 cm piece, hitched to a Panther Ausf. A, tactical number "612." The tank has Zimmerit of indeterminate pattern and a mottled camouflage scheme. *NARA*

In this view of a column of Panther tanks on a march, the closest tank is an Ausf. A with pistol ports on the turret, Zimmerit of the Maschinenfabrik Niedersachsen Hannover (MNH) type, and the jack stored horizontally below the exhausts. A bucket and what seems to be a crate are stowed between the exhausts.

Crewmen decorated with Iron Crosses assemble in front of a Panther Ausf. A produced by MAN between November 1943 and March 1944. It features the style of Zimmerit used by that factory, and a ball-type bow-machine-gun mount is present.

The "R02" marked on the skirts of this Panzerbefehlswagen Panther Ausf. A in Normandy indicates that it was assigned to a regimental executive officer.

Crewmen arrange local camouflage around the same Panzerbefehlswagen Panther Ausf. A in the preceding photo. On the turret is an insignia featuring a black panther leaping through a circle with a vertical lightning bolt superimposed over it.

A MAN-produced Panzerbefehlswagen Panther Ausf. A, tactical number "96," operates along a dusty road. It has the horizontally stored jack below the exhausts, a carrier for a jerry can next to the right exhaust, and three racks made of angle irons on the rear deck.

A combat photographer crouching alongside a road next to a cargo truck catches a glimpse of a Panther Ausf. A. The action of the track guides has worn the paint off the outer rims of the inner road wheels and has polished the steel to a high sheen.

A photo of infantrymen poised to fire their weapons aboard a Panther Ausf. A provides an excellent view of the cast cupola. Seven periscopes with armored hoods were set into the cupola. The object on the cupola to the front of the forward periscope is a vane sight. *NARA*

A Panther Ausf. A is at a crossroads in the countryside. The road sign to the front of the tank includes a reference to Caën, a settlement in Upper Normandy. The vehicle has a mottled camouflage scheme and a severely damaged right front mudguard. *NARA*

A Panther Ausf. A advances along a narrow lane. Daimler-Benz-type Zimmerit is present on the tank. Also present are the ball-type bow-machine-gun mount and a single aperture on the mantlet for a monocular sight.

Two Panther Ausf. A tanks roll along a street in the city of Debrecen, Hungary, during the battle for that city in October 1944. Several of the skirt panels are missing on the lead tank; the side of the turret is covered with spare track sections. *Bundesarchiv*

On August 7, 1944, a force of Panther Ausf. A tanks and other combat vehicles from the 1st and 2nd SS Panzer Divisions mounted a counterattack against elements of Gen. George S. Patton's 3rd Army around Avranches, France. The force ran into roadblocks manned by infantry and the 823rd Tank Destroyer Battalion, which was equipped with 3-inch M5 guns, a potent antitank weapon. That battalion knocked out a number of German Panthers and armored vehicles in the firefight, including this Sd.Kfz. 251 Ausf. D half-track and two Panthers, which were put out of commission by antitank guns under Lt. Tom Springfield north of L'Abbaye Blanche. The Panther in the foreground was built by Daimler-Benz, while the one at right was built by MAN. In the background, above the turret of the Panther to the left, is a US 3-inch M10 gun motor carriage. Library of Congress via Kevin Hymel

The same two Panthers and Sd.Kfz. 251 Ausf. D are viewed from another perspective. The driver's hatch door on the Panther to the right had been blown from its mounting and was hanging over the top of the glacis. The number "378" is painted on the rear of the turret of the Panther to the left. *Library of Congress via Kevin Hymel*

On another Daimler-Benz Panther knocked out by Lt. Springfield's 3-inch guns, both tracks are missing, the right idler is dangling almost to the ground, and the forward set of bogie wheels on the right side has been blown off. The section of spare track on the turret is akilter. *Library of Congress via Kevin Hymel*

A Panther numbered "328" in a curious location on the turret and gun mantlet is lying where it was knocked out by Springfield's guns, with an American 3-inch M10 GMC visible in the background. This MAN Panther belonged to SS-Panzer-Regiment 1, which at the time assigned the platoon leader a turret number ending in 5, with the remaining vehicles numbered upward from there until the last ended in 9. The light-colored area on the sponson of the Panther appears to represent damage from a projectile that hit the armor and Zimmerit antimine coating but failed to penetrate. Farther to the rear of the sponson is a smashed jerry can. *Library of Congress via Kevin Hymel*

Another view of the two Panthers and Sd.Kfz. 251 Ausf. D half-track lie in the fog in front of Lt. Springfield's position. In the two days of fighting in this area, US forces destroyed twenty-nine German vehicles, including nineteen tanks. The tank in the foreground is a Daimler-Benz unit. *Library of Congress via Kevin Hymel*

A Panther became wedged between a ditch and an embankment in front of Lt. Springfield's guns near L'Abbaye Blanche. A section of spare track is dangling from the left side of the turret. The defending US forces also employed bazookas and machine guns against the German tanks and vehicles. *Library of Congress via Kevin Hymel*

A kleines Kettenkraftrad passes a Panther Ausf. A, tactical number 233, poised next to a road sign for Via Casilina in Italy. This Panther has the single exhaust tailpipes and rough-textured Zimmerit divided into grids, apparently in the style practiced by Daimler-Benz. The crew evidently is not expecting imminent action, since the 7.5 cm gun is in its travel lock, a muzzle cover is present, and the antiaircraft machine gun is not installed on the ring mount on the cupola.

A Panther Ausf. A rolls through an intersection in a city in the Netherlands in 1944. (On the building in the background is a sign that reads "Voedingswaren," Dutch for "food.") The rough-textured Zimmerit characteristic of Daimler-Benz production is present on the tank. The object between the commander and the other crewman on the turret appears to be an antiaircraft machine gun with a cover over it. The travel lock is engaged to the 7.5 cm gun barrel.

Two Panther Ausf. A tanks of the Panzer Lehr Division were knocked out near Le Désert, France, in 1944. The Panther on the left has MNH Zimmerit, and the outboard aperture for the binocular gunsight on the mantlet has been plugged. *NARA*

A member of the US 4th Infantry Division peers inside the driver's hatch of a Panther Ausf. A that was knocked out by American bazookas during the fighting in Normandy on July 16, 1944. The blown-off hatch door is leaning against the left mudguard. *NARA*

A dead crewman of a knocked-out Panther Ausf. A lies under a cover in front of his tank outside of St.-Pois, France, on August 5, 1944. Grid-type Zimmerit, rather roughly scored, in the style of MNH application, is visible on the glacis. *NARA*

A pair of Panther Ausf. A's of the 11th Panzer Division were photographed in Dieuze in September 1944.
The tank in the foreground has camouflage netting stretched over its glacis.

A Panther Ausf. A knocked out by high-velocity rockets fired by a British Typhoon fighter near Bretteville, Normandy, in the summer of 1944 lies upside down on the road.

Refugees near Villedieu, France, inspect a Panther Ausf. A, tactical number "321," knocked out by US gunners in the summer of 1944. Areas of the MAN-style Zimmerit have spalled off the left-rear facet of the turret. *NARA*

This Panther Ausf. A on a city street in a subtropical setting was knocked out. Several bullet or shrapnel holes are visible in the skirts and the container for the bore-cleaning staff. A letterbox bow-machine-gun cover and binocular main gunsights are visible. *Patton Museum*

The same Panther Ausf. A in the preceding photo is seen from the rear. The exhausts and the hatch cover on the rear of the turret have been blown off, and the antigrenade screen of one of the ventilators on the left side of the engine deck is bent upward. *Patton Museum*

British and American troops explore a knocked-out Panther Ausf. A, with the blown-off turret to the right. Features worthy of notice include the pistol port on the rear of the turret with a large number "2" next to it, and the Demag-style ridged Zimmerit. *Library and Archives of Canada*

From the Normandy Campaign on, German Panzer troops dreaded the P-47 Thunderbolt fighter-bombers, which they dubbed "Jabos." Here, P-47 pilots get a rare chance to observe their handiwork close-up on a Panther Ausf. A they struck in July 1944. *NARA*

The white, powdery coating toward the rear of the turret and the blackened mantlet suggest that this Panther Ausf. A had been knocked out and burned. Judging by the Zimmerit pattern, this vehicle was constructed by MNH between September and November 1943. *Library and Archives of Canada*

An Allied soldier examines a German overcoat left behind in the wreckage of a Panther Ausf. A. Blown-off road wheels are lying in the grass in the right foreground. *Library and Archives of Canada*

At an unidentified battlefield in Europe, Allied soldiers inspect a knocked-out Panther Ausf. A. Numerous projectile holes are present on the turret, hull, and wheels, and sizable chunks of armor have been gouged out of the turret and the sponson. *Library and Archives of Canada*

Allied forces encountered this abandoned Panther Ausf. A in a thicket at an undisclosed site. The access door for the engine compartment is open. A grid-type Zimmerit pattern is visible, and the left exhaust is flanked by cooling pipes for the left manifold. *Library and Archives of Canada*

Allied armored troops conduct a postmortem on a Panther Ausf. A. Though the rear of the hull was torn up, it had the early Ausf. A arrangement, with two exhaust pipes, brackets for a horizontally stowed jack below the exhausts, and no tow coupling. *Library and Archives of Canada*

Allied tank troops pose for the camera on the same Panther Ausf. A shown in the preceding photo. This was a MAN-manufactured, early Ausf. A vehicle with a cast cupola, letterbox bow-machine-gun cover, and binocular main gunsight in the mantlet. *Library and Archives of Canada*

Whenever possible, Allied troops would look through a captured Panther tank for any items of intelligence value, and this highly feared and respected tank always was an object of curiosity. *Library and Archives of Canada*

Canadian soldiers look over a Panther Ausf. A that has fallen into their hands on the road to Hochwald, Germany, on February 27, 1945. The left rear storage bin has come loose from its upper holders and is dangling from its lower holders, parallel to the ground.

A destroyed Panther Ausf. A lies among the ruins in front of the cathedral at Cologne, Germany, on March 7, 1945. On the previous day, from a position in the square before the cathedral, this tank had engaged in fierce duels with several US tank units, which included Sherman tanks and one of the new T26E3 Pershing tanks. It was finally the Pershing that knocked out the Panther.

The Panther Ausf. A knocked out in the cathedral square in Cologne on March 6, 1945, is viewed from a slightly different angle. Thanks to several US Army cameramen in the vicinity on March 6, this tank duel was extremely well documented photographically with both movie and still cameras. The turret of the Panther was turned to the right side subsequent to the battle. *NARA*

Panther Ausf. A

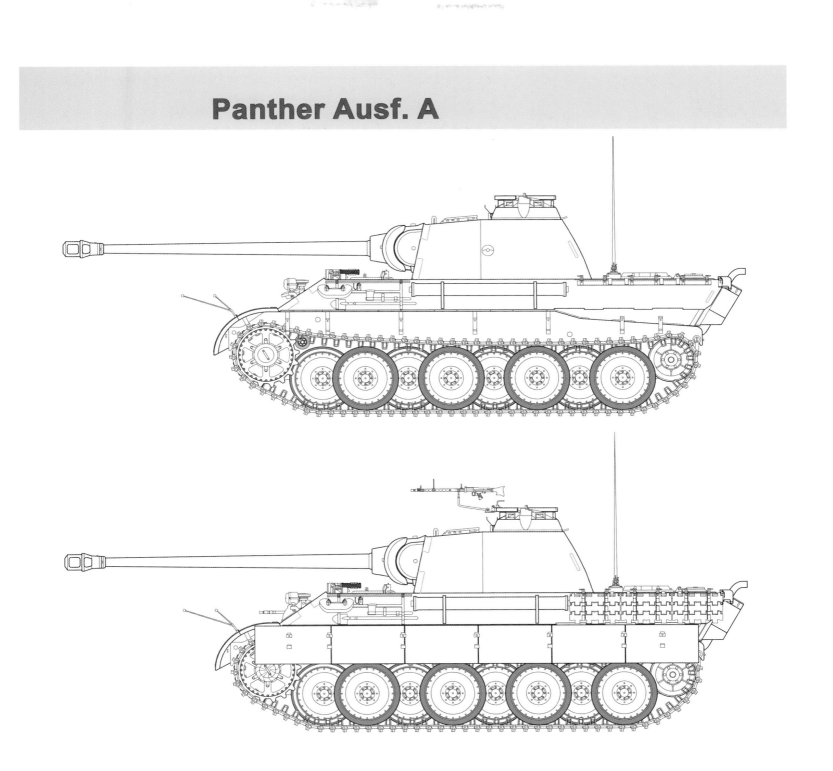

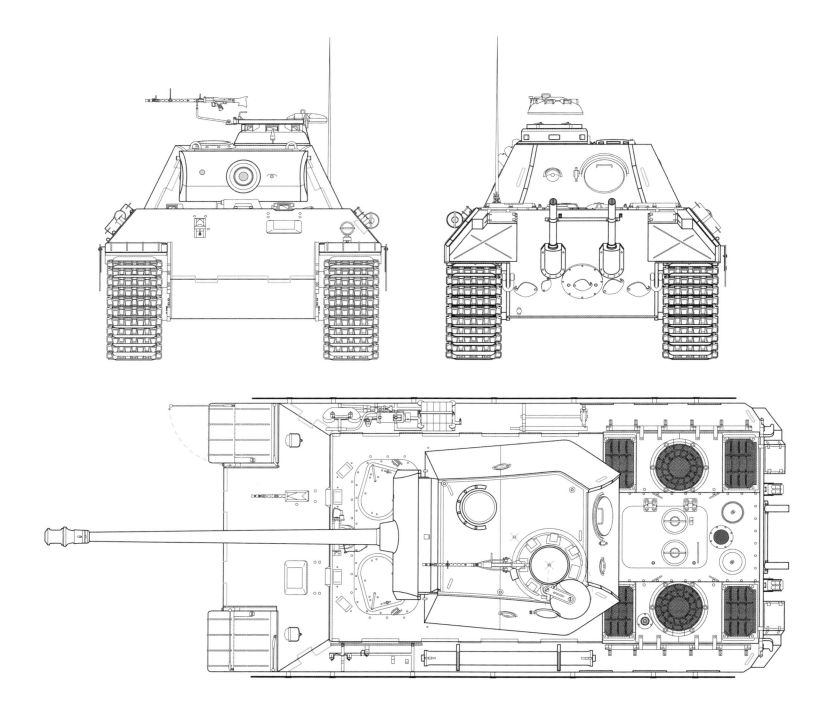

Sometimes, tactical numbers on Panthers consisted of only two digits, indicating the number of the platoon and the vehicle. Such was the case with the Panther Ausf. A from Panzer Regiment "Großdeutschland" in June 1944. A lightly sprayed Olivgrün camouflage has been applied over the Dunkelgelb base color. A small Stahlhelm, the symbol of this regiment, is painted on the turret to the rear of the tactical number.

No additional camouflage colors have been applied to the Panther Ausf. A of the commander of 2nd Platoon, 2nd Company, 5th SS Panzer Regiment "Wiking," in Poland in 1944. Cross-hatched Zimmerit is present on the turret and the hull.

The Musée des Blindés, in Saumur, France, preserves this Panther Ausf. A, painted to replicate a vehicle of the Panzer Lehr Division in France in 1944. The turret was cannibalized from another chassis. The driver's visor is in the open position. *Massimo Foti*

Pock marks, evidently from machine gun rounds or shrapnel (or both), are present on the 7.5 cm gun barrel. Reportedly, the Zimmerit as seen here was applied during the restoration of the tank.
Massimo Foti

Mounted on the sponson is the storage tube for the bore-cleaning equipment for the 7.5 cm gun. An angle iron along the top of the tube provided additional rigidity. Following the practice of German Panther units in wartime, spare track sections are liberally stored on the turret and sponson. *Massimo Foti*

On the center and the forward end of the right sponson are empty racks for storing tools and equipment, including a track-tensioning tool, sledgehammer, wire cutters, jack block, fire extinguisher, C-hook, track-change cable, and starter crank. *Massimo Foti*

The Canadian War Museum, in Ottawa, Ontario, added a restored Panther Ausf. A tank to its collections in 2008. After the Allies captured the tank in World War II, it was shipped to Canada in early 1945 and displayed at Canadian Forces Base Borden until it was donated to the Canadian War Museum. Restoration of the tank at the museum took two years, consuming 4,000 hours. *Author*

The left sprocket is seen close-up. Around the rim are thirty-two countersunk, locking hex nuts, each of which is secured with a cotter pin. An armor disc was welded onto the hub cap. *Author*

Several of the interleaved bogie wheels are depicted. Each wheel has twenty-four hex bolts around the rim, for attaching the tire-retainer ring, located on the reverse side of the wheel. The tires were vulcanized rubber, with steel wire embedded in them for extra strength. Square-pattern Zimmerit is on the side of the hull. *Author*

Near the front of the left sponson is a rack with a shovel, an ax, and a tow-cable holder. Above the shovel blade are two cylindrical holders for a C-hook. *Author*

Two periscope guards are on the roof to the front of the driver's hatch. The gunner's sight aperture on the left half of the mantlet has been plugged. *Author*

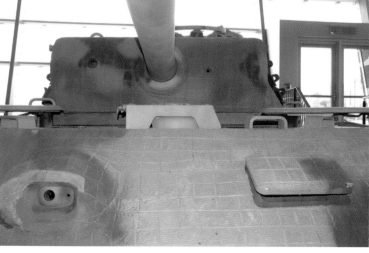

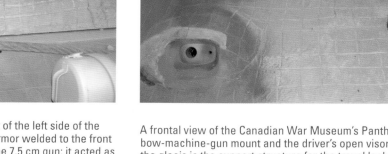

Details of the 75 mm gun mantlet and the forward part of the left side of the turret are displayed. The small, trapezoidal piece of armor welded to the front of the turret was designed to limit the depression of the 7.5 cm gun; it acted as a stop when the bottom of the mantlet made contact with it. A similar stop is on the right side of the turret front. The device with the small operating handle on the access panel on the driver's compartment roof is a lock, to prevent the driver's hatch door from swinging when the vehicle is in motion. Author

A frontal view of the Canadian War Museum's Panther Ausf. A includes the bow-machine-gun mount and the driver's open visor. Behind the top center of the glacis is the support structure for the travel lock for the 7.5 cm gun. During production of the Panther Ausf. A, the radio operator / bow gunner's forward periscope was deleted, as seen here, leaving him only his side periscope, which is visible to the left. *Author*

In a view from the left rear of the same tank, the cupola, the rear of the turret, and the engine deck are featured. A lifting ring is to the rear of the cupola, and the round hatch on the rear of the turret is ajar. Three of the periscope hoods on the cupola are visible. *Author*

Along the top of the sponson are U-shaped brackets with L-shaped retainer pins for holding spare track sections. On each side of the deck are one round fan cover and two rectangular cooling-air inlet vents. On the center of the deck is the engine-access hatch, with two air-intake covers on it. To the rear of the hatch are, *left to right*, the radiator filler, the mount for an air-intake snorkel, and the fuel filler. The fillers had caps, not installed here. *Author*

The round fan covers are secured to lugs on the engine deck with hex bolts. The two air-intake covers on the engine-access hatch have handles, for turning the covers in order to lock or unlock them. These covers were removed when the engine was running. *Author*

The left fan cover and the two engine-air inlet covers are viewed from a closer perspective. To the far left is a radio-antenna base. *Author*

The two filler openings and the mount for a snorkel are seen from the left rear of the engine deck. On the rear of the hull are the tailpipes, the right storage box, and the lifting hook built into the rear of the sponson. *Author*

The left-rear cooling-air inlet vent is viewed close-up. During wartime service, screens were bolted over these vents to keep out foreign objects and hand grenades. For that purpose, a bolt hole was tapped at each corner of the vent. *Author*

Flanking the left tailpipe, which is dark colored, are two cooling pipes for the engine-exhaust manifold. At the bottom of the right tailpipe is its armored guard. *Author*

The American Heritage Museum, in Stow, Massachusetts, preserves this Panther Ausf. A from the Jacques Littlefield Collection. The tank was retrieved from a salvage yard in eastern Europe, where it had been submerged underwater for some forty years. It was in very poor shape when recovered but was beautifully restored by Littlefield's team. *Chris Hughes*

When the German crew abandoned the Panther, they detonated an explosive charge inside the vehicle, to prevent the captors from using it. The turret was so severely damaged that much of it was rebuilt from steel. *Chris Hughes*

The roof and engine deck of the Littlefield Panther Ausf. A were rebuilt during the restoration. Other components such as the bottoms of the sponsons and bulkheads also were of new construction. The turret ring was a new old-stock replacement procured in France. *Chris Hughes*

Because of the explosive charge that the crew detonated to destroy the vehicle, and the decades the vehicle spent in the water, much of the interior components of the Panther had to be removed and new parts and components installed. This is a view through the driver's hatch, showing his seat, steering levers (*left*), and transmission and transmission shift lever (*top*). To the lower right is one of four suspension dampers. *Chris Hughes*

The transmission gearshift lever was positioned close to the transmission case, making it somewhat difficult for the driver to manipulate. According to reports, it was common for drivers to bang their right elbows when shifting. *Chris Hughes*

This is a driver's view of the right side of his compartment, including the seven-speed, manual synchronized transmission with the instrument panel on it. The panels include a speedometer/odometer, tachometer, water and oil temperature gauges, fuse panel, engine-fire warning indicator, and starter switch. On the transmission next to the gearshift lever is a shifting-pattern placard. The two boxes to the right were for a microphone and headphones. *Chris Hughes*

The driver's instrument panel is shown close-up. Atop the transmission is radio equipment, with controls facing to the right, toward the radio operator's station. The device with the red knob toward the left is an electric gyroscopic compass. *Chris Hughes*

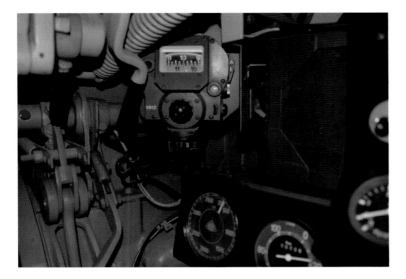

The driver's electric gyroscopic compass is shown close-up. Toward the top of the compass is the black course-setting dial, directly below which is the yellow gyro dial. The red knob below those dials is for locking and setting the gyro. *Chris Hughes*

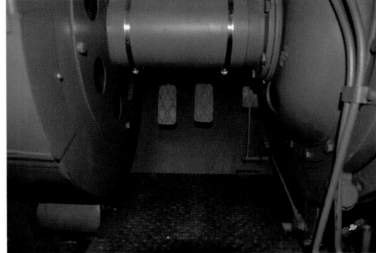

Below the cover for the left output shaft are, *left to right*, the clutch pedal, foot brake, and accelerator pedal and its linkage. To the left is the left steering-brake cover, and to the right is the left side of the controlled differential. *Chris Hughes*

As seen from the driver's position, facing forward, at the top is the vision port with bulletproof glass block; to the rear of the glass block is the driver's front periscope. To the upper right is the driver's side periscope. To the right are the instrument panel, transmission, and gyro compass. To the lower front are the differential, final drive, and left steering brake. *Chris Hughes*

The front periscope for the driver, the black device at the upper center, is seen from the driver's position, with the visor and glass block to the lower front of it. *Chris Hughes*

As seen from the driver's perspective, at the center is the side periscope and to the right are the front periscope and the glass block behind the driver's visor. The black hoses to the right of the periscope provide hydraulic fluid to the power-steering system. To the left, spare periscope prisms are in a storage box. *Chris Hughes*

The radio operator / bow gunner's hatch door is in the open position, as seen from above the hatch. The cylinder below the door contains its operating mechanism. When opened, the door lifted above its resting place and swung outward. To the upper right is the lock that immobilized the door when open. In the sponson to the far right are electrical transformers for the radio sets. *Chris Hughes*

In the radio operator's compartment, to the left is part of the radio set, to the right of which are the headrest and sight for the MG 34 bow machine gun (*center*). At the bottom is the radio operator's seat. The red object to the right is the top of a suspension damper. The hydraulic hoses to the upper right are associated with the power-steering system. *Chris Hughes*

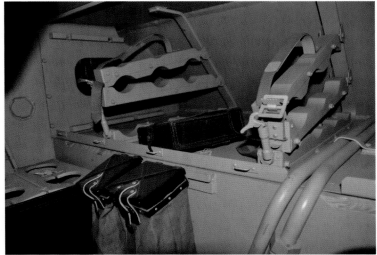

The radio installation in the Panther Ausf. A at the American Heritage Museum is seen from the radio operator's perspective. The set was designated the FuG 5 SE 10 U and FuG 2 EU, with two Ukw.E.e. FM receivers stacked to the left and a 10 W.S.c. transmitter to the right, with a radio antenna connection box above it. This combination of sets was used in Panthers assigned to platoon and company leaders. To the right are the gunsight and headrest. *Chris Hughes*

There were two 7.5 cm ammunition-storage locations in both of the sponsons. This is the forward one in the right sponson, with two folding racks for eight rounds of 7.5 cm ammunition, stored in three tiers. Straps and clamps were used to hold the racks together when ammunition was stored on them. To the lower left are racks for vertically storing 7.5 cm ammunition. *Chris Hughes*

Two ammunition pouches for the MG 34 bow machine gun are stored on the right side of the radio operator's compartment. The long canister with the strap attached is a carrier for two spare machine-gun barrels. *Chris Hughes*

Another 7.5 cm ammunition storage bay in a sponson is shown, with a vertical rack with a 7.5 cm round in it in the foreground. Pouches for 7.92 mm ammunition for the machine guns are below the sponson racks. *Chris Hughes*

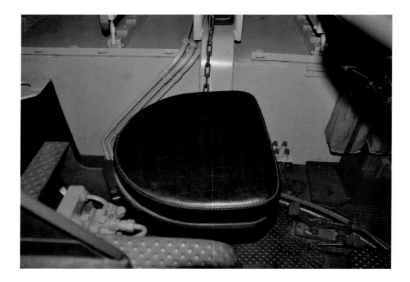

Above the left side of the floor of the turret is the gunner's seat, which was mounted on a pedestal. The red device on the floor to the front of the seat is the gunner's foot pedal for firing the coaxial machine gun. *Chris Hughes*

Below the box to the left is an Abschmierplatte, or lubrication plate, where lubrication lines could be refilled from one location. Near the right-rear corner of the fighting compartment is the upper part of a suspension damper. To the lower left is the floor of the turret. *Chris Hughes*

Above the floor to the front of the gunner's seat and machine-gun firing pedal are two large pedals made of diamond plate, at the center. By rocking these pedals, the gunner controlled the speed and direction of the traverse of the turret. *Chris Hughes*

The right rear of the fighting compartment is seen from a different perspective, showing, left to right, the suspension damper, two machine-gun ammunition pouches, a rack for three rounds of 75 mm ammunition, a round clamp for a Zerstorpatrone (demolition charge), and a fire extinguisher. *Chris Hughes*

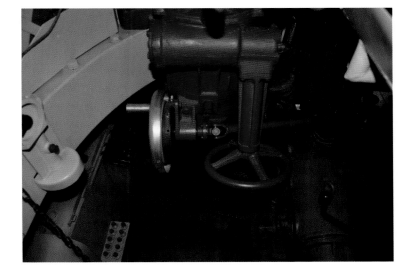

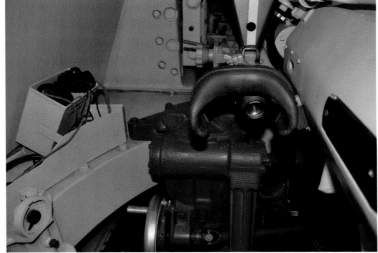

To the front of the gunner's station in the turret is, *left*, the elevating handwheel, with the horizontally oriented traversing handwheel to its right. The Panther was provided with both manual and powered traversing systems; the manual control usually was used for small variations in traverse. *Chris Hughes*

The gunner's telescopic sight and face guard are above the traversing gear. The scope used in the Panther Ausf. A was the TZF 12a. The flared object with a vertical white stripe above the scope is its support. To the lower left is a Seitenrichtungsanzeiger (azimuth indicator), with a single dial showing the lateral position of the turret. The scale that was part of the indicator is not present. Above the indicator is a bin for a microphone and headphones. *Chris Hughes*

The gunner's handwheels are viewed from under the breech of the 75 mm gun. The shaft from the elevating handwheel runs to the elevating gear, out of view to the right. The shaft of the traversing handwheel runs upward to the traversing gearbox, at the center of the photo. The shaft with the universal joint that is attached to the right side of the traversing gearbox transmitted power to that box from a hydraulic transmission on the floor of the turret. The red mechanism and the steel cables to the right are parts of the pneumatic equilibrator for the 7.5 cm gun. *Chris Hughes*

The traversing gearbox of the turret was driven manually or by a hydraulic transmission, which is viewed from the left side, with the right traversing pedal to the bottom. The red cardan shaft with a universal joint toward the upper left transmits power from the hydraulic transmission to the traversing gearbox. To the right is another red universal joint, which took power from the engine driveshaft to drive the hydraulic transmission. The handle on the side of the transmission controlled the speed of powered traverse. *Chris Hughes*

The breech of the 7.5 cm Kw.K. 42 L/70 gun is at the center, with the recoil guide to the left and the 7.92 mm MG34 coaxial machine gun, ammunition pouch, and ammo chute to the right. To the upper left is the cupola, and to the upper right is the ventilator exhaust fan. The curved pipe around the left side and rear of the breech was part of a bore-extraction system, which blew compressed air into the gun tube to drive propellant gases out. *Chris Hughes*

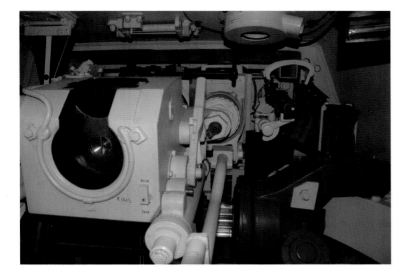

On the right side of the 7.5 cm gun breech is the breech-operating lever. Visible between the gun breech and the elevating gear are the elevating rack and pinion. *Chris Hughes*

A change from the Panther Ausf. D to the Ausf. A was the addition of an auxiliary drive for the turret, the red object to the far right. Next to it is the turret lock. *Chris Hughes*

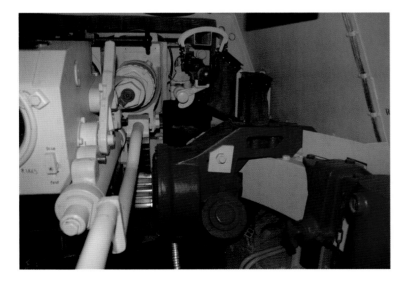

At the center, to the right of the 7.5 cm gun breech is the dark-red elevating gearbox, to the front of which is the coaxial MG 34 and its ammunition pouch and chute. *Chris Hughes*

At the center is the loader's periscope, to the left of which is the electrical exhaust ventilator. To the upper right is the weld bead between the right side of the turret and the roof. *Chris Hughes*

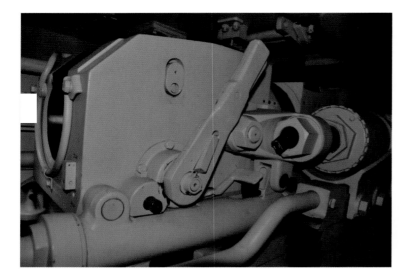

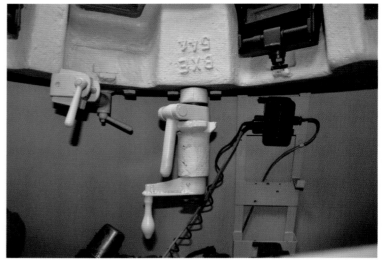

The breech of the 7.5 cm Kw.K. 42 L/70 is viewed from the right side, showing the position of the breech-block-operating lever. To the right is the recoil cylinder; on the other side of the gun is the recuperator cylinder. On the roof to the right of center is part of the interior travel lock for the gun. A fitting on the top of the gun was engaged to that device during travel. *Chris Hughes*

In a partial view of the cupola from below, at the center is the operating mechanism for the cupola hatch door, which both raised the door, with the lower crank handle, and swung it to the side, with the upper, folded, handle. To the upper right is one of the seven periscopes located around the cupola. The interior of the cupola has a rough-cast texture. On the bottom of the cupola to the left of the hatch controls is a bracket for a T.S.R. 1 periscope. *Chris Hughes*

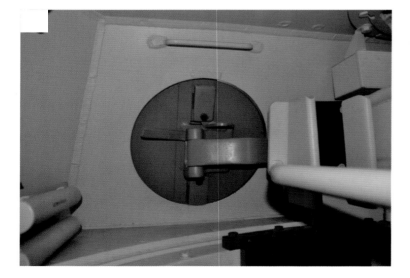

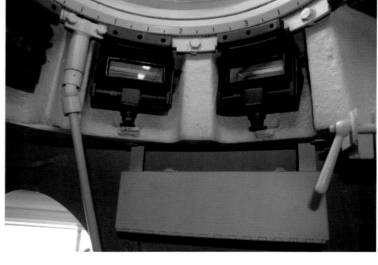

The rear turret hatch is viewed from the loader's position. To the left of the top of the hinge is the locking lever. The hatch door was locked in place by sliding bolts on the vertical centerline of the door. A grab handle is welded to the rear of the turret above the hatch. *Chris Hughes*

In another view of the interior of the cupola, with the rear hatch of the turret to the lower left, three periscopes are in view. Toward the left is a driveshaft for causing the azimuth scale near the top of the cupola to turn in unison with the traversing of the turret. *Chris Hughes*

A restored Panther Ausf. A Panzerbefehlswagen (armored command vehicle) is exhibited in the Deutsches Panzermuseum, in Münster, Germany. After World War II, the Swedish army procured this Panther for testing purposes, returning the tank to the *Panzerlehrbrigade* at Munster in 1960. The *Panzertruppenschule* restored the vehicle in the 1980s; eventually a new MTU diesel engine was installed, and the tank is in running condition. *Massimo Foti*

The Panther Ausf. A Panzerbefehlswagen at Munster has a single, angled periscope for the radio operator. A Notek blackout headlight is mounted on the right side of the glacis, and a Bosch headlight with its slotted cover installed is on the left side of the glacis. Noticeable on each side of the mantlet are circular shapes with a horizontal, ridged texture. Similar circles, minus the ridged texture, are faintly visible in several of the photos of the Panther Ausf. G at Bovington, presented later in this book. The circle on the right side has a plug in the aperture for the coaxial machine gun. *Massimo Foti*

Although difficult to discern, a *Sternantenne* (star antenna) is mounted on the engine deck to the rear of the turret. This antenna has prongs radiating from the top of the antenna mast and was associated with the FuG 8 30-watt transmitter. Also on the engine deck is a rod antenna. *Massimo Foti*

In a left-side view of the Panther Ausf. A Panzerbefehlswagen at Munster, the object on the engine deck directly to the rear of the turret is a detachable boarding ladder. *Massimo Foti*

The engine exhausts on the Munster Panther Ausf. A Panzerbefehlswagen have been repositioned out of their normal order, with a single tailpipe on the left side, and a tailpipe with an exhaust-manifold cooling pipe on each side on the right side. This swapping-around of the pipes sometimes occurred on Panthers in French service after World War II and on museum specimens. *Massimo Foti*

The jack is stored vertically between the engine exhausts. On the round engine-access plate below the jack is a tow coupling. Heat shields are on the inner sides of the storage boxes. These are sometimes seen on wartime photos of Panthers, often with an X-shaped stiffener stamped into the surface. *Massimo Foti*

CHAPTER 3

Panther G: The Most Abundant Cat

As the war progressed, the armor protection of the Panther was found to be inadequate. Meanwhile, the vehicle's drivetrain was overtaxed due to the increase in the vehicle's weight far beyond original specifications. At the same time, Allied air attacks against Germany's industrial centers were becoming increasingly effective. As early as 1943, design work began on the Panther II, which was to be a more heavily armored, easier-to-produce tank, having increased parts commonality with the Tiger tank.

Ultimately, aside from one prototype, the Panther II was not produced, but the lessons learned were incorporated into a new Panther model: the Ausf. G. The side armor of the Panther G was increased to 50 mm, while armor in other areas (including the bottom and lower front hull), was reduced slightly to offset the weight gain caused by the thicker side armor.

Other changes further simplified the Ausf. G's production, which began in March 1944 at MAN, with later transitions to

Daimler-Benz and MNH. From the time the Ausf. G entered production in March 1944 until production ended, just over 2,950 of the tanks were completed.

A few Panthers went on to serve in post-WWII armies, notably fifty Panthers of the French army's 503e Régiment de Chars de Combat, and thirteen Panthers of Romania's 1st Armored Brigade. It is also worth pointing out that the British Army captured the entire Maschinenfabrik Augsburg-Nürnberg (MAN) factory, although the facility was damaged. The Royal Electrical and Mechanical Engineers went to considerable effort to relocate the tools and equipment needed for Panther production to Laatzen (south of Hannover), before resuming production with MNH employees. There they made nine Panthers and twelve Jagdpanther tank destroyers for test purposes—but did not continue production either for use in British Army armored units or for sales to other governments. However, the British-built Panthers were the last of the type to be completed.

The Panther Ausf. G retained the same turret as the Ausf. A but had a newly designed hull in which the wedge-shaped armor at the bottom rear of the each sponson and the related stepped floor of the sponsons were replaced by the straight bottom edge for the sponsons and a straight sponson floor. Seen here is Panther Ausf. G, chassis number 121052, completed by MAN on or near September 22, 1944, featuring steel-tired 800 mm road wheels, no Zimmerit, and an early example of an installation of *Kampfraumheizung* (crew-compartment heating), evidenced by the raised object on the engine deck. *Patton Museum*

Panther crewmen adjust local camouflage or enjoy a break in a courtyard on the Western Front in 1944. The nearer vehicle, an Ausf. G, has a debris guard over the mantlet, a modification instituted in August 1944, and appears to have MAN-style Zimmerit.

Tank crewmen and infantrymen congregate on a Panther Ausf. G in France in 1944. The rear panel of the right armored skirts is missing, revealing just below the spare tracks the thin fender on the hull to which the tops of the Ausf. G–type skirting abutted.

On some Panther Ausf. Gs, such as this one with MAN-style Zimmerit produced between June and August 1944, the cylindrical container for the bore-cleaning brush and staff was moved from the left side of the vehicle to the rear of the engine deck.

Panther tanks are being transported on railroad flatcars. The tank to the front of the partially visible vehicle in the foreground is a Panther Ausf. G. The exhausts have welded guards, introduced in May 1944, with a Zimmerit coating, and sheet-metal shields for the tailpipes, a June 1944 modification. The Zimmerit on the rear storage bins is the variety with vertical ridges and diagonal scratch marks.

Two crewmen of a Panther Ausf. G, heavily camouflaged with tree branches, wait expectantly as thick smoke billows up from an explosion to the front during a battle in France in 1944. This vehicle has cast-steel exhaust guards and sheet-metal tailpipe shields, both of which have Zimmerit coatings. The Zimmerit is of the rough-textured pattern associated with Daimler-Benz's application style.

A MAN Panther Ausf. G produced between June and August 1944 has halted on a road in France in 1944. The spare road wheel on the turret is an early one with sixteen bolts around the perimeter. The thin fender is visible and damaged toward the front.

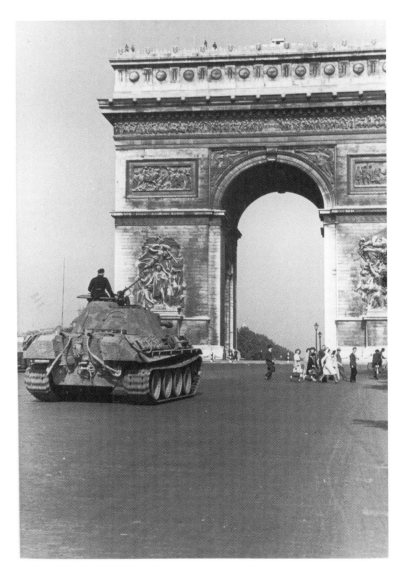

A Panther Ausf. G of 1st SS Panzer Division Liebstandarte SS "Adolf Hitler" approaching the Arc de Triomphe in Paris in the summer of 1944 has the rough-textured, rather amorphous Zimmerit associated with Daimler-Benz's style of application. The handle on the turret's rear hatch was introduced in June 1944. Tow cables are attached to clevises mounted on the rear of the hull.

Another Panther Ausf. G photographed at the Arc de Triomphe exhibits the style of Zimmerit applied at the MAN factory and the type of welded exhaust guards that came into production in June 1944. Several of the right skirt brackets are visible. On the round access plate on the rear of the hull is the tow coupling for attaching tow bars: a feature introduced with Ausf. A.

Two Panzer crewmen by a tent and another one by the rear of a Panther Ausf. G take a break. The tactical number marked on the side of the turret is "I02," which stands for the vehicle of the assistant commander of the 1st Battalion. The full extent of the thin fender running along the side of the sponson is visible. Brackets along the underside of the fenders served to hold the skirts in place.

Two crewmen are engaged in a repair or replacement operation on the left track of a MAN-built Panther Ausf. G. Details of the Kgs 64/660/150 track are visible. The number 660 referred to the width of the track links, 660 mm. The number 150 represented the pitch, or the front-to-rear dimension of each link, in millimeters. There were eighty-seven track links per side. These tracks were a single-dry-pin type.

On September 20, 1944, a Panther tank from Panzerbrigade 111 has paused after advancing into Bures, France. The vehicle evidently had run into a hard object, bending back the lower front corner of the front panel of the *Schürzen*.

Panzergrenadiers are loading equipment on a Panther Ausf. G and are settling in for a ride to the front on the engine deck, during the Lorraine Campaign in September 1944. Zimmerit is present on the box-shaped armored guards around the bottoms of the tailpipes, and the sheet-metal shields around those pipes are battered.

In a photo taken an instant from the preceding one, Panzergrenadiers continue to arrange themselves on the engine deck of the same Panther Ausf. G. These tanks performed much battle-taxi service in the Lorraine campaign owing to a shortage of half-track personnel carriers.

German tank crews were adept at camouflaging their vehicles with foliage, to hide them from Allied fighter and fighter-bomber crews. The crew of this Panther Ausf. G from Panzerbrigade 111 has liberally arranged tree branches on and next to their vehicle during a stop in a town, likely Bures, in eastern France in September 1944. With the *Schürzen* not installed, the straight bottom of the sponson, a characteristic of the Ausf. G, is easily discerned.

Panther tanks, driving at long intervals to limit damage in the event of a sudden attack by Allied aircraft, are proceeding along a tree-lined road between Sarrebourg and Dieuze, France, in late September 1944. Hanging from the rear of the Ausf. G in the foreground are several items, including a small milk can.

A Panther Ausf. G is entering Bures, France, on September 26, 1944. The vehicle is painted in a three-color camouflage, likely consisting of Dunkelgelb (dark yellow), Olivgrün (olive green), and Rotbraun (red brown), but the two front panels of the *Schürzen* (skirts) do not match the third panel, suggesting that the front panels were cannibalized from another Panther, without an effort to repaint them to match.

The village of Bures, France, was a crossroads that frequently saw armies passing through it in the late summer and early fall of 1944. Here, the same Panther Ausf. G in the preceding photo, with the mismatched camouflage on the *Schürzen*, has paused next to a road sign indicating the direction and distance to Bures

Four Panthers serving with the 11th Panzer Division are gathered in Bures, France, in September 1944. Panzergrenadiers are embarked on all vehicles except for the one in the right foreground. Damage is visible on the rear storage boxes of both Panthers in the foreground.

A close examination of this photo of a Panther Ausf. G in the Lorraine Campaign in September 1944 reveals what is commonly known as an "ambush" camouflage pattern, which is particularly visible on the 7.5 cm gun barrel, the mantlet, the cupola, and the side of the turret. The vehicle is thought to have been from the 11th Panzer Division.

During a German counterattack against Gen. George S. Patton's 3rd Army in the Lorraine Campaign in France in late September 1944, a Panther Ausf. G with a tow cable hanging below its bow, right, is moving into the community of Bures while another Panther Ausf. G guards the road to the left. A broom is lying on the engine deck of the Panther to the left. Another Panther is on the road in the background between the tanks in the foreground.

In an image taken a moment after the preceding photo, the Panther Ausf. G with the tow cable dangling from its bow is passing the parked Panther Ausf. G in Bures. The MG 34 on the cupola of the Panther to the left appears to be at the ready, but ammunition is not loaded into it.

A heavily camouflaged Panther Ausf. G tank, *left*, is advancing past a parked Panther Ausf. G to the right, in Bures, France, in September 1944. The hinged hatch door of the radio operator of the vehicle to the left is partly open, and his head is visible above the hatch.

This Panther Ausf. G built in mid-September 1944 was equipped with an infrared searchlight and scope on the cupola. Particular to Daimler-Benz was the "ambush" camouflage, which featured small, contrasting splotches of paint on the Dunkelgelb, Rotbraun, and Olivgrün. *Thomas Anderson collection*

The turret of a Panther Ausf. G bears the tactical number R01, indicating the tank of the commander of a Panzer regiment. This vehicle features two distinct camouflage schemes, including an "ambush" camo used by MAN on the skirts. *Patton Museum*

A Panther Ausf. G with MAN-type Zimmerit is stuck in a roadside ditch in France on August 16, 1944. This tank was built before July 1944, since it lacks the three *Pilze* (sockets) for installing a boom on the turret roof. These sockets came into production in June 1944.

Three-color camouflage is present on a Panther Ausf. G with markings for the eighth vehicle, 2nd Platoon, 1st Company, SS Panzer Regiment 12, in the 12th SS Panzer Division "Hitlerjugend" in Normandy in 1944. The early-type mantlet lacks the chin that later was incorporated into the mantlet.

A Panther Ausf. G with the late mantlet with a chin is painted in the "ambush" camouflage introduced in the final months of World War II. This camouflage consisted of Dunkelgelb, Olivgrün, and Rotbraun, with small splotches of Dunkelgelb applied here and there on the two darker colors.

A distinctive three-color camouflage has been applied to this Panther Ausf. G, with Olivgrün areas with hard-edged Rotbraun borders applied over the Dunkelgelb base color on the main gun, the turret, and the upper hull. No tactical numbers or unit markings are present.

Canadian troops fired two PIAT (Projector, Infantry, Antitank) rounds into this Panther Ausf. G, knocking it out in Bretteville, Normandy, on June 20, 1944. The tank, with MAN-type Zimmerit, has features consistent with April–June 1944 production. *Library and Archives of Canada*

On this knocked-out Panther Ausf. G in Humain, Belgium, on December 28, 1944, jutting above the engine deck is a crew-compartment heater, an accessory that was installed on Panther Ausf. G assembly lines starting in October 1944. *NARA*

An M26 tractor manned by the 486th Ordnance Evacuation Company, 84th Infantry Division, 9th US Army, hauls a captured, trackless Panther Ausf. G through Geilenkirchen, Germany, on December 4, 1944. The tank has MAN-pattern Zimmerit. *NARA*

The same trackless Panther Ausf. G seen in the preceding photo is shown from a different perspective in the middle background as an M26 tractor tows it along a street in Geilenkirchen. American forces had knocked out this tank in the outskirts of that town. *NARA*

Members of the US 2nd Armored Division investigate a snow-caked Panther Ausf. G on the outskirts of Grandmenil, Belgium, on January 4, 1945. The crew of the Panther abandoned it when a cartridge became jammed in the 7.5 cm gun. *NARA*

A US Army Sherman tank of the 2nd Armored Division rolls past a knocked-out Panther Ausf. G outside Grandmenil, Belgium, on or about January 2, 1945. Over the driver's periscope is a sheet-metal rain guard, a feature introduced in August 1944. *NARA*

A 9th Armored Engineer Battalion Caterpillar Model D7 tractor with a bulldozer pushes an abandoned, snow-plastered Panther Ausf. G out of the way along a road near Manhay, Belgium, in early January 1945. *NARA*

A British or Commonwealth soldier contemplates the chewed-up front mudguard of a Panther Ausf. G in a town in Europe. What appears to be MAN-type Zimmerit is visible. The running gear is destroyed. On the mantlet is a monocular gunsight aperture. *Library and Archives of Canada*

British or Commonwealth personnel inspect a captured Panther Ausf. G. This tank has the vertically stored 20-ton jack, introduced to production in February 1944, and the tow coupling on the round access hatch on the rear of the hull, introduced in April 1944. *Library and Archives of Canada*

An abandoned Panther Ausf. G of 9th SS Panzer Division sits in a street in Sterpigny, Belgium, on January 20, 1945. The vehicle has an overall dark appearance, with patches of snow on it. Toward the rear of the side of the turret is the tactical number "412." *NARA*

Another view of the tank above as Allied troops take stock of a knocked-out Panther Ausf. G, tactical number "135." Some of the troops are reading documents that likely they have discovered in the tank. The Zimmerit on the vehicle and the placement of the Balkenkreuz are MAN style. *Library and Archives of Canada*

An Allied soldier looks over an abandoned MAN-built Panther Ausf. G, tactical number "132," in Normandy in 1944. One of the armor skirt panels was blown off and is leaning on the front of the turret. The vehicle has characteristics of April–June 1944 construction. *Library and Archives of Canada*

A Sherman ARV tows a captured Panther Ausf. G in the winter of 1944–45. The 7.5 cm gun and mantlet have been removed from the turret. The Balkenkreuz on the front of the sponson is situated in accordance with MAN factory painting practices. *Library and Archives of Canada*

British or Commonwealth crewmen are staffing this captured and operational MAN Panther Ausf. G in Europe in late 1944 or early 1945. This vehicle has a debris guard over the mantlet and a standard mantlet without the "chin" introduced in September 1944. *Library and Archives of Canada*

A GI looks over a knocked-out Panther Ausf. G at Kelberg, Germany, on March 11, 1945. The presence of a crew heater on the engine deck and a ring mount on the cupola indicates that the manufacture of the vehicle was completed between October 1944 and January 1945. *NARA*

A Free French soldier prepares to spray a new coat of paint on a captured Panther Ausf. G in a city in France on September 18, 1944. The tank was being prepared for dispatch to Paris as a war trophy. Faintly visible on the roof of the turret in line with the center of the cupola from this angle is one of three Pilze (sockets) welded to the roof to hold a jib boom for heavy-lifting and repair operations in the field. These sockets began finding their way onto Ausf. G turrets in the factories in June 1944. The prominent ledge above the mantlet is the front edge of the debris guard, introduced to production in August 1944. *NARA*

The tactical number "111" is faintly visible through the soot on the turret of this Panther Ausf. G. When it was knocked out, the flames caused most of the rubber tires on the road wheels to burn. A "chin" mantlet with extended bottom to deflect shots is present. *NARA*

A US Army CCKW cargo truck has just passed a Panther Ausf. G knocked out by elements of the 2nd Armored Division near Brissonville, Belgium, on December 29, 1944. This Panther features a crew-compartment heater and welded guards for the exhaust pipes. *NARA*

An antitank team of the 1st Infantry Division inspects a Panther Ausf. G knocked out by a bazooka near Fernegierscheid, Germany, on or around March 26, 1945. The most conspicuous damage is the torn-up sprocket. This Panther is equipped with the chin mantlet. *NARA*

Parked next to a Tiger tank is a Panther Ausf. G, tactical number "135." The placement of the Balkenkreuz at the front of the sponson is the specific practice of the MAN factory, and the Zimmerit is typical MAN style, with vertical ridges set inside grids. Patton *Museum*

This Panther Ausf. G exhibits characteristics in keeping with a completion date of April to June 1944, since it lacks the Pilze (sockets) on the turret roof for a jib boom. The placement of the Balkenkreuz and the pattern of the Zimmerit are of the MAN style. The Zimmerit consists of vertical ridges laid out in horizontal rows, not discernible grids. The cylinder for storing the bore-cleaning brush and staff is battered, and the cap on the front end is detached. Of interest is the fact that the tactical number, "308," has been painted over a larger, former tactical number, 126. *Patton Museum*

Besides producing new Panthers, MAN also remanufactured battle-weary Panthers regardless of manufacturer. Incoming tanks were dismantled on a disassembly line, then reassembled using new or refurbished mechanical components. This Panther G hull, coincidentally built by MAN, has been stripped of many of its internal components. *NARA*

A US Strategic Bombing Survey team found this Panther Ausf. A on wooden stands in a factory. The thickness of the glacis armor is apparent in the area where the bow-machine-gun ball mount is absent. *NARA*

With the bombed-out, massive Vereinigte Fränkische Schuhfabriken (United Franconian Shoe Factories) rising in the background, a trio of combat-worn Panthers await unloading from railcars at the MAN plant. The rebuild for which they were sent to Nürnberg will never come. *NARA*

This Daimler-Benz-built Panther was among several found on railcars at the MAN plant when it was captured in April 1945. Heavy bombing raids had completely disabled the plant, and even rebuilding tanks in the facility had been stymied as a result. *NARA*

Another US Strategic Bombing Survey photo depicts a Panther turret, as found on a stand in a factory. The turret basket is visible below the top of the stand. A steel lifting sling is attached to the lifting eyes on the turret roof. *NARA*

All the Panthers were powered by either the HL210, shown here, or the HL230 TRM gasoline engine. Designed by Maybach, the engine was produced by Maybach, Auto Union, and Daimler-Benz. *NARA*

A Panther tank photographed for the United States Strategic Bombing Survey on a flatcar in the yard of the MAN plant shortly after the war reportedly had been knocked out in combat. A large hole is present in the sponson, and the left track is rolled up to the front of the vehicle. *NARA*

Panther Ausf. G

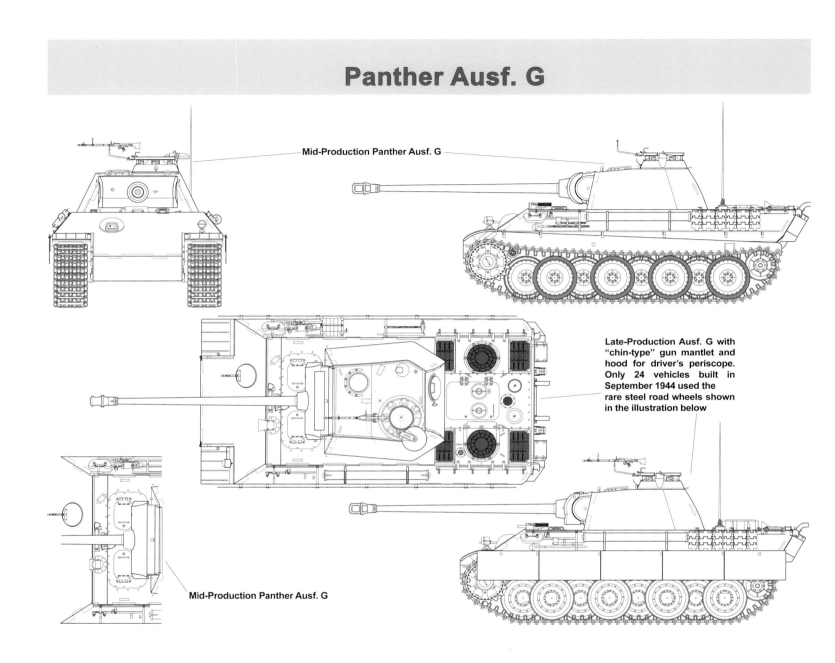

Mid-Production Panther Ausf. G

Mid-Production Panther Ausf. G

Late-Production Ausf. G with "chin-type" gun mantlet and hood for driver's periscope. Only 24 vehicles built in September 1944 used the rare steel road wheels shown in the illustration below

The Tank Museum, Bovington, England, preserves this very late Panther Ausf. G, the eighth of a number of Panther Ausf. Gs to be completed shortly after the fall of Nazi Germany by the British 823rd Armoured Troops Workshop of the Royal Electrical and Mechanical Engineers (REME) at a plant in Laatzen, Germany, that had fabricated subassemblies for Panther tanks. The Laatzen factory was a subsidiary of one of the Panther manufacturers, Maschinenfabrik Niedersachen-Hannover (MNH). The 823rd Armoured Troops Workshop was mandated to assemble as many Panther tanks as possible from remaining stocks of parts and components, for purposes of testing the tanks and comparing them with British tanks. As far as is known, the British completed only eight of these Panthers. *Massimo Foti*

The impressions of circles, discussed earlier among the photos of the Panther Ausf. A Panzerbefehlswagen at the Deutsches Panzermuseum, Munster, Germany, are faintly visible on each side of the mantlet of the Panther Ausf. G at Bovington. The fenders show some damage, and a single panel of *Schürze* (skirt) is installed on the right side of the tank. *Massimo Foti*

The camouflage scheme seen here, applied in 2008, replicates a very late-war scheme, as then understood, consisting of red primer, Dunkelgelb (dark yellow), and thin borders of a light-colored paint. *Massimo Foti*

The front cap is missing from the canister for the bore-cleaning equipment on the left sponson, exposing a semicircular part with three holes in it, for storing three spare antenna sections. Beginning with Ausf. G production, the Bosch headlight was moved from the left side of the glacis to the left fender. *Massimo Foti*

Several late-production features are visible in this left-rear photo of the Panther Ausf. G at Bovington. A Warmluftbeheizung (crew compartment heater), introduced in October 1944, is the large shape on the engine deck. Flame-suppressor exhaust mufflers are present on the rear of the vehicle. Finally, the rear storage boxes had vertical stiffeners stamped into their rear faces, instead of the X-shaped stiffeners of the earlier boxes. *Massimo Foti*

During the Ardennes Offensive in December 1944, the Germans sent into battle a number of Panther Ausf. G tanks disguised as US M10 tank destroyers. Here, US soldiers inspect one of these vehicles that has lost its left track and become mired along a road. *Patton Museum*

The left side of the mantlet of this fake M10 tank destroyer based on a Panther Ausf. G has been shot up. Panels were applied to the Panther to replicate the angular M10, and US insignia and bogus unit markings were painted on these vehicles. *Patton Museum*

The left rear of the turret of the same fake M10 is viewed close-up. The turret was traversed toward the right to about the two o'clock position. The rear of the Panther's turret is to the right, and the fake side plate is to the left. *Patton Museum*

The badly damaged false mantlet of the same imitation M10 seen in the preceding photo is viewed close-up. The shape of the stock Panther Ausf. G mantlet without the shot trap on the bottom is under the ripped sheet metal of the false mantlet. *Patton Museum*

The roof of the same fake M10 is seen from above, facing to the rear. To the left rear of the turret, the Panther's cupola has been removed and a flat, two-part hatch has been fitted over the cupola's opening. A crude US insignia is painted on. *Patton Museum*

CHAPTER 4

Panther F:
The Panther That Wasn't

The Panther Ausf. F was an experiment to mate a newly designed Schmalturm (narrow turret) to a Panther Ausf. G chassis. One of these experimental vehicles is shown in an August 20, 1944, photograph. No tools were mounted on the chassis for these experiments. *Thomas Anderson collection*

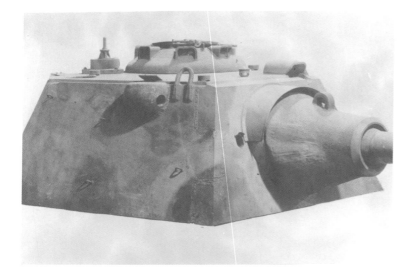

The Schmalturm had a narrow front, presenting a smaller area to frontal fire. The nearly conical mantlet was designed to deflect shots and prevent a shot trap that would permit rounds striking the bottom of the mantlet to penetrate the hull roof. *Patton Museum*

The sides of the Schmalturm feature small loops for fastening camouflage materials. The commander was provided with a cupola that was lower than the one on the Panther Ausf. G, and was equipped with seven periscopes with armored hoods. *Patton Museum*

A curved rain deflector was attached to the front of the turret over and to the sides of the mantlet. The left lifting eye had broken off. Jutting from the upper part of the sides of the turret were guards for rangefinder objectives. *Patton Museum*

Unlike the standard Panther commander's cupola, the hatch of which rose and then swung to the side, the commander's hatch on the narrow turret was hinged at the back. At the rear of the turret is an escape hatch and a pistol port. *Patton Museum*